WORKING WITH DANES

TIPS FOR AMERICANS

KAY XANDER MELLISH

Publisher: BoD – Hellerup, Denmark
Printing: BoD – Norderstedt, Germany
ISBN: 978-87-4302-768-3

For June 5 and September 17

Introduction

If you're an American who is about to do business in Denmark, the Danes you meet will probably know a lot more about your country than you do about theirs.

US movies, TV, and streaming services are all popular in Denmark, and Danes also like US music and fashion. Some have passionate opinions about US politics. Many Danes have visited the US or even spent an exchange year there during high school.

On the other hand, if Americans hear about Denmark at all, they often hear information that is not entirely correct.

For example, Denmark is not "socialist" – it's a social welfare state, a free-market economy in which the voters have agreed to be taxed very highly in exchange for universal health care and tuition-free universities.

(Anyone who shops in a Danish supermarket will get a sense of what the national 25% sales tax does to the price of groceries.)

Denmark also isn't the cheerful utopia some people on the left would like it to be.

Everyone must work and pay taxes to keep the welfare state financed. And social services are closely measured and monitored to keep people from riding for free.

The country has some of the toughest immigration

rules in Europe, rules that have forced many well-meaning Americans out of the country, including some married to Danes.

Fewer people than Houston

Denmark is *small*. With fewer than six million people, it has a lower population than metropolitan Houston.

Yet because of its high educational levels and long history as a trading nation, it still produces regular innovations in pharmaceuticals, engineering, and green technology, not to mention world-famous Danish design.

Having lived and worked in both the US and Denmark, I have a great fondness for both countries. I hope you'll enjoy working in Denmark and with the Danes.

Kay Xander Mellish

Copenhagen, Fall 2020

Why Denmark is a great place to do business

Denmark is a lovely, quiet, gentle country with well-educated people who speak excellent English.

Infrastructure is superb, with well-paved roads and buses and trains that run mostly on time. Internet access is almost universal, and digital initiatives have made the Danish government largely paperless.

Corruption is minimal[1], a key factor in persuading the populace to pay some of the world's highest taxes.

It's less upsetting to see a substantial chunk disappear from your salary when you believe the funds are being used for roads, schools, and hospitals, not to line some corrupt politician's pockets.

---

1   *Denmark is one of the world's least corrupt countries, according to Transparency International's 2019 Corruption Perception Index.*

Employee relations

The tax system in Denmark is much more transparent than the US system, and legal systems in general tend to be simpler and easier to understand.

So are the rules about working conditions. Maximum working hours, required vacations, and termination procedures for salaried employees are outlined in a national law that every corporate HR person knows backwards.

Conditions for hourly employees generally follow rules outlined by their unions, who make umbrella agreements with the companies in their sector.

Unions are also the first touchpoint when it comes to employee disputes, even for knowledge-sector employees.

That means less running back and forth to HR. And wrongful termination suits and discrimination filings are less common in Denmark than they are in the US.

In general, Denmark is much less litigious, which means much less record-keeping and monitoring is required.

Work-life balance

Denmark is known for its work-life balance, which applies to managers as well as their teams.

Most Danish offices are empty by 4pm, as both male and female employees rush home to pick up their children and prepare a fresh dinner. (They often log on again after the kids are in bed to finish up assignments.)

Time off is sacred in Denmark: full-time workers get a minimum of five weeks' vacation per year and usually take two to three weeks in a row during the summer.

Many companies close down entirely during the last two weeks of July and between Christmas and New Year's.

If you choose to stay in the office at this time, you'll find there's not much to do besides tidy your desk or make plans for busier times ahead.

"Merchant Harbor"

Although its emphasis on a well-rounded life is part of its appeal, Denmark is a place that respects business.

The name *Copenhagen*, the country's capital and largest city, translates literally to "merchant's harbor."

For hundreds of years, ships have been sailing in and out with goods and people under the flag of trade.

If you're just arriving to do business in Denmark, you're the newest thread in the centuries-old tapestry of Danish commerce. Welcome.

Two words to better understand your Danish colleagues

Two words that will help you understand your Danish colleagues both begin with A, and you will see a lot of them in this book.

The first is *authenticity*. Danes have a visceral dislike for anyone or anything who pretends to be something they're not.

This will apply to you when job hunting or on the job – don't exaggerate your capabilities or promise influence you don't have – and to your products.

The concept of overselling your product, or promoting features that are perhaps not entirely proven yet, is totally unacceptable to the Danes.

Danish business, like Danish society, is based on trust.

Trust is usually given by default, but if you lose your credibility it will be almost impossible to get it back.

Dislike of authority

The second is *anti-authoritarianism*.

This is a society that has an intense dislike for authority and elites.

Advanced programs for "gifted children" are rare; instead, talented kids are expected to help their struggling classmates.

A degree from a prestigious university is also not the crucial differentiator that it is in the US. There are only eight universities in Denmark, all of them excellent.

In the workplace, everyone gets to have their say, even the most junior employees.

Don't show up in Denmark expecting automatic respect based on your title, your position, or your academic credentials.

Acting like visiting royalty is a sure way to antagonize the Danes.

Better to be friendly, humble, and down-to-earth — which is how the real-life Danish Royal Family conducts itself.

The sacred value of time

Nothing is more sacred to a Dane than their time.

Danes value time more than they value money or prestige. What they want to use that time on is up to them: family, hobbies, or the unquenchable Danish passion for fixing up their homes.

Never waste a Dane's time. Someone who is tardy is seen to be untrustworthy, which is why it's important to never be late to either a social appointment or a business meeting.

A 10am meeting really is a 10am meeting – not a 10:05 meeting. 10am sharp. (Americans sometimes unconsciously arrive late to show how busy and important they are. *"Sorry I'm late! I was on the phone with the President."*)

Also, a little friendly chatter before getting down to business is fine, but keep it short.

In general, the Danes prefer to work first and socialize later.

Taking time off work

In the US, taking time off work can be seen as a little selfish, as if you're not really doing your part for the team.

But for Danes, one of the main purposes of work is to finance one's time off. They will take every single day of their allotted vacation time, often at their bosses' insistence.

If they're at all sick, they will stay home, and disturbing them (even if you have an angry customer on the line) is simply not done.

Most companies also allow parents to take a day or two off to care for a sick child, and Danish law provides for extensive parental leave when a child is born or adopted.

Some companies will hire a specific "parental leave cover" person for the nine to twelve months a staffer will be away.

There's no point in bothering a Danish colleague on parental leave. They usually have no idea what's going on back at the office, and they like it that way.

Job-switching is common

On a macro level, Danes don't want to waste time doing a job they don't enjoy.

Job switching is common – employees in Denmark

change jobs more often than in any other country in Europe[1] – and the small size of the Danish market means your best employees have plenty of contacts among your competitors.

That's why it's vital to make sure your Danish employees feel engaged and challenged on the job.

They won't stay with your company purely out of fear, because the Danish social system gives them a soft pillow to fall on.

Work must have meaning

You also won't make Danes happier just by giving them a glittering job title.

Even a raise, while appreciated, will mostly vanish into the jaws of the tax department.

To keep good Danish employees, you'll have to make them feel that their work has meaning and that their contribution is valued.

God arbejdslyst! is an age-old phrase you'll sometimes hear Danes saying to each other as they embark on a project.

It translates to, "Enjoy your work!"

---

1   *According to 2018 statistics from Eurostat, the EU's statistical bureau, 11.8% of Danes age 25-64 changed jobs in the previous year. In nearby Sweden, the rate was 6.2%.*

Danish names

Looking up your Danish colleagues' names in a directory can be a little tricky if you don't know the inside rules of Danish names.

A large percentage of your colleagues will have similar last names – Hansen, Nielsen, Jensen. These are old composites meaning "son of Hans", "son of Niels", and "son of Jens".

Trying to distinguish between so many people with the same name is as frustrating for the Danes as it is for you, particularly since many people also have similar first names.

If you're searching for someone called Niels Jensen or Jens Nielsen on LinkedIn, the Danes' favorite social media network, you'll find dozens of people named precisely the same thing.

Note the middle name

That's why it's key to focus on the middle name – say, Niels *Smedegaard* Jensen. These family names often mean a lot to the Danes, since they harken back to a special farm (*gaard*=farm) that may be in the living memory of older relatives.

For that reason, you may find Danish colleagues referring to the man you know as Niels Jensen as *Niels Smedegaard*, particularly if there is another Niels Jensen on the payroll. After work when they are sharing a beer, they may even just call him *Smedegaard*.

Women and names

Danish women sometimes take their partner's name when they marry, and sometimes don't. (And they often do not marry at all; it's common to have long partnerships and several children without the benefit of a ceremony.)

At any rate, you're spared the worry about whether to call someone Miss, Mrs., or Ms., since these terms have almost entirely died out in Denmark, except on airplane tickets.

If you're addressing communication to a Danish woman, just use her full name: *Anne-Sophie Mølgaard Nielsen*.

Should you need to distinguish her from another woman with a similar name, you can add her occupation up front: *IT Specialist Anne-Sophie Mølgaard Nielsen*.

Extra letters in the alphabet

Danish has three letters that don't exist in English: Æ, Ø, and Å. They are placed at the very end of the alphabet, which is why you'll find any word beginning with these letters at the back of the dictionary.

Æ can be replaced with AE and Ø with OE if you lack a Danish keyboard.

Å is sometimes replaced with the double-letter A: the large city of Århus even officially changed its name to Aarhus to make it easier for internationals to type.

The Danish "flat hierarchy"

If you ask the Danes what they like about their business culture, they're sure to mention the *flat hierarchy*.

What they mean is that a management pyramid that might have ten or more layers in a hierarchical country like Japan has only two or three layers in Denmark.

The flat hierarchy is a virtue born of necessity: salaries are high in Denmark, so middle managers are expensive.

And because Danes aren't supervised or monitored as much as Americans, middle management isn't as necessary.

Just ordinary guys and gals

With so few layers, the opportunities for promotion and a better title are slim, which can be kind of a drag if you're the sort of person who is motivated by advancement.

In fact, to admit that there's any hierarchy at all is somewhat embarrassing to the anti-authoritarian Danes.

This is why top managers will go out of their way to show they are just ordinary guys and gals, carefully putting their coffee cup in the dishwasher after the team breakfast.

And when it's time for yet another company boozefest, the big boss is expected to drink and dance right alongside everyone else.

Talking to top management

This presumed access to top management also means that employees may want to share their thoughts directly with the big boss.

One local head of a US Fortune 500 company told me that his Danish employees were driving him crazy.

"Whenever they have an idea, they come straight to me," he said. "I tell them: You've got a direct supervisor, talk to that person. I can't keep track of input from almost 200 people."

The flat hierarchy and loneliness

One aspect of the flat hierarchy that isn't always discussed is that it can lead to silo thinking and loneliness.

The hierarchy is so pared-down that each employee is doing something different, and nobody really knows what anyone else is doing.

The skeleton crew supervising them are so busy themselves that they don't have time to monitor everything their team is up to.

And so the silo'ed employee works on, unsure if what she is doing is really vital to the company's mission or if it is just *pseudo work*[1], the topic of a wildly popular book about Danish office life.

---

[1]   *Pseudoarbejde, by Anders Fogh Jensen and Dennis Nørmark*

Flexicurity and unions

Another word you may hear when Danish business culture is discussed is *flexicurity*, a combination of "flexible" and "security".

This means that in Denmark it's relatively easy to hire and fire employees, but the social welfare system gives them a soft cushion to fall back on.

Litigation between former employee and employer happens occasionally, but it's not common in Denmark.

Union umbrella agreements

An important part of flexicurity is unions, which are much less antagonistic towards management than they are in the US. Unions play a big role in corporate life, even for knowledge workers.

Some workplaces include employees from many different unions, often based on their area of education –

the engineers in one union, the communications team in another.

But certain industries, such as banking, have umbrella agreements with a single union. Everyone who works at a bank gets the benefits worked out by the Financial Services Employees Union Denmark.

The union as the touchpoint for complaints

When an employee has a complaint – whether it's harassment on the job, an unsafe working environment, or a payment dispute – the union is usually the first touchpoint, not the government or HR department.

At big companies, the union will have a *tillidsrepræsentant*, a sort of shop steward who is appointed from among the employees. That person will be the first contact for a staffer with a complaint.

At smaller firms, the employee may call the union directly and have the union call you.

Employee contract review

Unions are powerful, and union lawyers are up on all the latest developments in labor legislation.

They generally know enough not to get involved in a losing case, so if you hear from one of them concerning an employee, it's worth listening carefully.

In addition, some potential hires will ask for 48 hours

to run an employment contract past their union before accepting the job. This is standard, and not necessarily the sign of a troublemaker.

Finally, should you want to fire an employee, a union rep will help that employee negotiate the best possible termination agreement.

In fact, the shop steward is usually brought into the room as a witness if a union member is getting the chop.

Turn down the volume!

One of the great differences between Danes and Americans is their idea of what a good person is.

Americans think a good person is energetic, upbeat, friendly, confident, and able to fix things.

That's why Americans tend to bounce into a room with big smiles, big body language, and booming voices.

This can be a bit much for the Danes, who are by nature on a somewhat lower volume setting.

What is a good person?

For Danes, a good person is calm and reliable, doesn't stand out too much, and has a sharp sense of irony poised to take down anyone who thinks themselves high and mighty.

In a worst-case scenario, Americans can misinterpret this low-wattage approach as sourness and negativity – and to be fair, sometimes it is.

But more often, it's just a culture of self-restraint and a belief that a quality person, like a quality product, is self-evident.

Be yourself, but quieter

This is not to imply that Americans should hide who they are. Authenticity is important.

Just be aware that all that puppyish enthusiasm can be overwhelming to your Danish colleagues.

If you're accustomed to cranking the smile meter with a one-to-ten setting up to an 11, you may want to turn it down to a four to match your Danish team.

Selling to Danes

While Danes admire the dynamism and creativity of American business, they do not envy the American way of salesmanship.

The idea that somebody should pretend to be your very best friend until he succeeds in selling you something is upsetting to them.

Instead, Danes believe that a good product sells itself.

Don't exaggerate

Appealing to the emotional side of buying will be an immediate turnoff for your Danish contact.

So will exaggerating your product's benefits or overall success. Exaggeration is never appreciated in a Danish context; it corrodes trust.

Your Danish buyer is by nature skeptical. Deep product knowledge and a readiness to explain specific benefits will allow your product to "sell itself."

"Not invented here"

For a society that is generally open to the outside world, there's still a deep conviction that the Danish way is best.

You'll notice an enormous number of products with names beginning with "Dan" – from DanEgg in the supermarket to DanDryer for your hands in a public restroom.

Fruits and meats are often proudly identified as being of Danish origin, presumably because the farmers use fewer chemicals and take better care of their animals.

And someone with a degree from a Danish university will almost always be taken more seriously than someone with a non-Danish degree. (A Dane with an international degree on top of her Danish degree will be taken even more seriously.)

That means that as a non-Dane, you'll already be one step behind, and two steps behind if your product would benefit from a Danish-language interface and doesn't have one.

Extra research

As an outsider, it's particularly important to research how your product fits into the Danish market, whether or not there are any tax or regulatory angles in a Danish context, and how it will co-ordinate or compete with products already in use in the buyer's industry.

You will not be able to sell based on charm alone in Denmark.

The Danish calendar, and holiday weeks to avoid

Most online calendars contain a hidden setting for "week numbers," in which the first week of January is Week 1, running through Week 52 at the end of December.

These week numbers are widely used in Denmark. Your Danish colleagues may suggest a conference in Week 18 or inform you that they will be on vacation in Weeks 29, 30, and 31.

It's actually a clever system which gets rid of clumsy expressions like *How about the week beginning Monday, October 3?*

At any rate, you may want to activate the week number setting in your calendar so you know what your Danish colleagues are talking about.

Predictable vacation periods

Danes love their five weeks of vacation, but the good news is they tend to take them at predictable times, particularly if they have children in school.

The first big vacation week is Winter Holiday in mid-February (Week 7 or 8) when many families take off for a ski trip elsewhere in Europe. Denmark has few hills steep enough to ski down.

In spring comes Easter. The official public holidays stretch over five days, but many employees take extra days off before or afterwards, usually to open up the family's summer house.

Several one-day public holidays are sprinkled through the spring and are often used for teenagers' confirmations (a big deal in Denmark) or weddings.

Three-week summer holidays

Kids in Denmark get just six weeks off during the summer, from July to mid-August (Weeks 27 to 32). Their parents can be counted on to take at least three weeks off in a row during this period.

Fall holiday in October (Week 42) is a popular time for urban trips to Berlin, Budapest or New York. If you're visiting any major city during this period, you can expect to hear Danish spoken.

Finally, the Christmas season lasts from December 23 to January 2, with just a couple of poorly attended business days in the middle.

Plan your business around the holidays

Examine the Danish holiday calendar and confer with your Danish employees well in advance before planning a sales campaign or product launch.

Your team will not be open to re-arranging their vacations for you.

Asking anything more than a skeleton crew to work during these periods will be taken as the sign of a manager who "doesn't understand Denmark."

Good morning. Good day.

The English term *good morning* can be used anytime up until 11:59am, but in Denmark, *good morning* runs out around 10am, at which time it is succeeded by *good day* or a simple *hej*.

Saying *good morning* after 10am can sound sarcastic, as if you are implying that you're happy your colleague has finally turned up for work.

Watch out for "half seven"

Danes use military time – 16:00 instead of 4pm – when they want to be precise, but they may say *4 o'clock* in casual use.

Something to watch out for is that "half seven" in Danish corresponds to 6:30, while "half past seven" in English is 7:30.

Keep this in mind when making plans with Danish colleagues and clarify times if needed.

Managing Danes

Traditional top-down American bosses can struggle at first to lead their teams in Denmark, where the management culture is very different.

In a country where equality is king, merely thinking that you're in authority over someone else is a slightly comic position.

You may be the one who makes the final decision about products, staffing, and strategy, thinks the Danish employee, and *you might be the one who sits across from me at the annual employee evaluation*, but **don't think you're better than me.**

Social welfare confidence

Part of this is the Danish social welfare system: "management by fear" is less effective when employees have access to two years of unemployment payments should they decide to leave their jobs. And their medical care and children's college prospects will be entirely unaffected.

But a bigger factor is the Danish child-raising and educational system. Children are raised to challenge their parents and their teachers, who they call by their first names.

In fact, the traditional Danish grading system (recently revised) used 11 for a flawless paper – but it was possible to achieve an even better grade, a 13, if your work was so spectacular that it taught the teacher something new.

Having an incentive to bust apart the status quo is the very basis of Danish innovation culture, and one of the reasons this tiny country punches above its weight on the world stage.

Everybody's opinion counts

What it means for you as a boss, however, is that nobody is going to carry out your orders just because you say so.

You need to earn respect, which isn't granted automatically.

Your team will expect to be consulted, expect to have their input collected, their questions answered, and their ideas acknowledged.

It's a much longer process, and if you see yourself as the kind of boss who likes to make snap decisions and turn on a dime, you may feel it limits you.

On the other hand, once you have worked hard to bring your team onside and earned their trust, they will follow you through fire.

Once they've committed to your project, it's their project too.

Keep calm in the workplace

Some American bosses have the unfortunate habit of shouting or losing their temper when things aren't going their way.

This baffles the peaceful Danes. Tantrums aren't a part of their culture, and they simply don't know how to react.

It's also hard for your Danish counterparts to judge how angry you really are. Does this outburst mean the relationship has been ruined forever? Or will they be expected to forget the whole thing once the problem has been resolved?

In a dramatic culture like the US, you may feel that a fiery outburst shows how much you care about the principle involved.

But to the Danes, you look immature and lacking in self-control.

Their weapon of choice is the sarcastic comment, or the passive-aggressive refusal to complete some task they secretly think is a waste of time.

"Jante Law" and why Danes underplay their skills

Many people believe equality is a desirable outcome. To make that happen, the short poppy must be helped to grow – and the tall poppy must be clipped off.

Tall poppy syndrome is what enforced equality is called in Australia, and in Denmark it's called the Law of Jante, after a novel from the 1930s.

Jante Law isn't a real law: it's a way of thinking in which it's considered good manners to underplay yourself, your skills, and your products.

At its best, this can result in delightful modesty and humility, an antidote to the constant self-promotion and pushiness that is part of American business life.

At its worst, Jante Law means petty envy and barely

concealed hatred directed towards people who are smarter or harder-working than you are.

It's no coincidence that most of the Danes I know who have chosen to move to the US have been energetic and innovative businesspeople, big personalities who didn't fit into little Denmark.

Danes undersell themselves

When doing business with Danes, be aware that they will probably be inclined to undersell themselves and their products.

It is anathema in Danish culture to promise something you cannot deliver, or to give your counterpart a "cat in a sack," an old farm expression for palming off a stray cat on someone who thought he was purchasing a tasty pig.

That means that Danes will under promise in order to make sure they are not overpromising.

You'll also notice this in Danish advertising, where no product is described as "better" or "the best."

This is because Danish marketing law only allows advertised products to be compared according to "specific, relevant, verifiable, and representative features," and *best* is rather subjective.

Generational change

There's a great deal of discussion in Denmark about

whether Jante Law is diminishing as new generations take their cues from the self-promotion common on social media.

While older Danes may have been brought up with the Jante Law basics – "Don't believe that you're anyone special" – younger people are more likely to be openly confident and careerist.

This is particularly true of people who work at the higher levels of US-affiliated companies.

Even so, an American-style elevator speech that makes you sound like a superhero will be poorly received by your Danish counterparts.

It's much better to speak calmly and humorously about your small successes and failures in business.

Admitting your imperfections makes you seem much more authentic – and much more likable – to the Danes.

Rating systems

A Dane recently told me about a misunderstanding he'd had with his American manager, who'd asked how things were going in his department.

"They're OK," the Dane said, meaning that the work was coming along in a satisfactory manner.

The US boss was concerned: he interpreted "OK" to mean that something was not satisfactory at all. If all were well, wouldn't his colleague have said, *"Great!"* or *"Super"* or even *"Excellent"*?

The American way of hyperbole meets its match in Danish understatement.

In Denmark, extreme understatement is a way of showing you're a good person with a sense of humor about yourself.

For example, a Danish man who has just won the Lotto and married the woman of his dreams might describe his mood as *slet ikke dårligt*, or "not bad at all."

Understatement vs hyperbole

If your company uses ratings systems for its products or managers, this culture of understatement may be reflected in the marks you get from Danish customers and colleagues.

A US customer might reflexively click on 10 when a company or product delivers everything it is supposed to deliver; anything less than 8 is a "bad score."

By contrast, a Dane might give 6 or 7 for the exact same performance.

They want to save the 10 for something really special.

Don't overdo it on the compliments

Americans love to give encouragement. They like to share the positivity. The US is, after all, the country that invented cheerleading.

But a boundless sea of compliments sounds artificial to the Danish ear.

From a Danish point of view, there are some things you are simply expected to do, such as the things you are hired for.

If you're doing them properly, no comment is required.

Constant applause

An American boss may feel she's being an inspirational leader by offering constant positive feedback – that she is bringing out the best in her people.

But her Danish team may feel they are being treated like children. *I am an adult professional. I don't need to constantly be applauded for doing my job.*

If you do give a compliment, it should be deeply felt, and you should be ready to elaborate on exactly what it is you found so impressive.

Cake to celebrate

That said, the Danes often say they envy the Americans' ability to celebrate success.

Success celebrations in Denmark are more modest. When things go well for your Danish team, it's traditional to bring a cake for everyone to share.

You don't have to bake the cake. Denmark has plenty of excellent bakeries, and to be honest most people would rather have a professionally made version.

Then choose a time in mid-afternoon, invite everyone involved, and perhaps make a two-minute speech re-iterating the highlights of the group's success.

And it is always a group success, even if everyone knows that one or two employees did most of the heavy lifting.

Celebrating bigger successes

For even bigger successes, such as an acquisition, companies sometimes throw a party with lots of food and lots of alcohol. (For Danes, it is not a party without a great deal of alcohol.)

If you plan to do this, announce it at least three months in advance.

Danes' calendars fill up quickly with family events and vacations, which is why Christmas parties should be announced in August at the latest.

Ambition and competitiveness

Most Danish schools do not give grades until children are 13 or 14, but there are occasional quizzes and such.

One day my daughter, who dislikes spelling, was pleased to find she'd done very well on a spelling quiz. She was eager to see how the other children had done and perhaps show off a little.

But when her teacher saw the kids discussing their marks, he quickly put a stop to it.

"Do not compare your score with the other children," he said. "Focus on your own work."

Do not compete against each other

If you've been brought up in an environment where competition is desirable and everyone knows who the top performers are, the Danish approach may be a bit of a shock.

Danish children – and adults – are not raised to compete against each other, and if you ask them to do so, they'll find it uncomfortable and distasteful.

This is a co-operative culture, where people generally work in groups and solidarity is seen as an important goal.

In a work environment, Danes will find it embarrassing if you single one employee out for doing well, or "hang out" an individual for doing poorly.

Competitive for products

That doesn't mean that Danes aren't competitive, but they are competitive for their product and service, not (at least openly) for themselves.

A survey[1] conducted of university students in 16 countries showed that only 49% of the young Danes surveyed hoped to go into management, compared to 77% of Americans surveyed.

Management responsibility in a corporate environment is seen as a headache by many Danes. Taxes will eat away much of the extra income, and a management job will require more hours at work, meaning less time with family.

On the other hand, entrepreneurship is popular.

1   *Building leaders for the next decade: How to support the workplace goals of Gen X, Gen Y, and Gen Z. Universum Generations Series, a collaboration with INSEAD Merging Markets Institute, the HEAD Foundation and MIT Leadership Center. 2017*

If I'm going to work crazy hours, think many Danes, *I'm going to start my own company,* either alone or with a group of like-minded colleagues. *Then the results of all that hard work flow back to me.*

Entrepreneurship and the "BMW Syndrome"

How big will those new startups grow? Some do very well, and some do just well enough to be sold to an enterprising buyer so the founder can go start a new company.

The "serial entrepreneur" is a staple of the Danish business media.

Other companies grow just big enough for the founder or founders to be satisfied with the income they have achieved and then plateau.

This is sometimes called the "BMW Syndrome." The point at which the founder can buy an expensive car (taxed at 150% of the purchase price) is the point at which the company tends to lose ambition.

Why do more when you've reached the limits of luxury in Denmark?

Gender equality in Denmark

Denmark has had two female prime ministers and about 40% of the people elected to the *Folketing*, their version of Congress, are women.

But when it comes to private industry, Danish women have one of the lowest participation rates in management in Europe. According to the OECD[1], about 26.5% of managers in Denmark are female, compared to 39.8% in the US.

It's not unusual to see a senior management team made up entirely of Danish males, with perhaps a Swedish or German male thrown in for diversity.

Most women work outside the home

That said, the majority of adult Danish women hold

---

1   *Organization for Economic Co-operation and Development 2018 statistics accessed from OECD.stat in June 2020.*

paying jobs. Stay-at-home parents are uncommon because the tax system makes it very difficult to survive on one income, even a hefty one.

For families with young children, the "Danish way" is for both parents to work full time and put the kids in government-run day care right after their first birthday.

Even the children of the Royal Family (including young Christian, the future King Christian XI of Denmark) did their time in government-run day care before moving into public schools.

Nannies are uncommon, although a few wealthy families have au pairs.

Danish men do housework

Danish men do more housework than any other men in the OECD nations, and are also deeply involved in childcare, although women still do more.

There's a certain expectation that even highly educated women with demanding jobs will bake buns (*boller*) from scratch, attend numerous parent meetings at the school or kindergarten, and plan cozy birthday parties for their children.

It's common for women with full-time jobs and young kids to be diagnosed with stress and take sick leave from work.

Time off vs career

Denmark's generous parental leave is supposed to be shared between parents but is, in practice, taken mostly by mothers. (That said, for creative-class men in Copenhagen and Aarhus, taking a few months of paternity leave has become a status symbol.)

I can say from personal experience that it's wonderful to have a paid year off to tend to and bond with a new baby.

A vast industry has sprung up to help new parents enjoy their child's first few months, offering baby swimming, baby music, baby yoga, and even baby psalm-singing at the local church.

Local governments even set up "mothers' groups" with five or six local mothers who have given birth at about the same time. They can share their various baby triumphs and troubles with other woman experiencing similar milestones.

Sometimes these groups click and the mothers and children become lifelong friends.

Interrupts the trajectory

But this paid time off does interrupt women's career trajectories, particularly because many Danish women choose to have two or three children in their 20s and 30s while their male counterparts are building business experience.

How much of the gender differences in management

is discrimination, and how much is personal choice? It's a difficult question to answer.

Some women try to split the difference and do part-time work while they raise their families, although in practice this can often morph into full-time work with part-time pay.

Don't expect chivalry

The blurring of traditional gender roles in Denmark has also eliminated traditional chivalry.

If you're a woman dating a Danish man, don't expect flowers, gifts, or to have him pick up the check for a romantic dinner.

In fact, if you're interested in a Danish man, it's always a good idea to take the initiative yourself.

Even in a non-dating environment, don't assume that a man will open doors for you or that a man will get up to let you have his seat on public transport when you have been standing (uncomfortably swaying) for a dozen stops.

A Danish man knows you can stand on your own two feet.

Differing concepts of privacy

A Danish friend was giving a speech to an industry organization in the US. As she introduced herself, she listed her professional accomplishments, then noted that she was 44 years old, divorced, and the mother of two wonderful children.

Some of the Americans in the audience were shocked. Why in the world would she reveal her age? And shouldn't her family status be her own personal business?

First of all, your age is rarely private in Denmark. Your birthdate, including the year, makes up the first six numbers of your CPR number, which is somewhat of a Social Security number on steroids that gives you access to everything from tax-funded medical care to library books.

It's very difficult to lie about your age to anyone who

has access to your CPR, right down to the guy who signs you up for your fitness center.

(The good news is that Danes tend to be more relaxed about signs of aging than Americans are. Photos of middle-aged celebrities, for example, often leave crow's feet and moles unretouched.)

Secondly, sharing family information in a business context is common in Denmark. Danes also frequently add it to their CV's to give a potential employer insight into themselves as a whole person.

Casual nudity

Casual nudity is also much more accepted in Denmark than it is in the US. Nude winter swimming in the chilly Danish harbors is a national passion, and even at the local swimming hall you'll be expected to get clean in the shared shower *without* your suit before diving in.

On the other hand, some things are more private in Denmark than they are in the US.

The standard mug shot you'll see in the US media whenever someone interesting has been arrested is unknown in Denmark.

Criminals are rarely pictured or named in the media, even after conviction. Images of a suspect on the loose are shared with the public only if the crime is very serious.

Why EU privacy laws are important

In addition, Denmark is part of the European Union's overall directive on privacy, which means you may have trouble accessing some websites from the US that don't comply with that directive.

The EU's privacy directive also includes the "right to be forgotten," which means that if you as an individual appear on someone's website and don't want to be there, you can approach them directly and ask for the item to be taken down.

I've done this myself a couple of times for old video interviews that were no longer relevant, and in both cases the item disappeared within an hour.

The downside is that other people can do this too, so if you find an important or delicate piece of information online that you'd like to refer to later, take a screen shot.

Privacy law affects marketing

EU privacy law will also affect your marketing efforts: there are very strict rules about what type of information you can send and who you can send it to.

Get used to seeing the initials "GDPR," which is what the General Data Protection Regulation is commonly called, and to hearing why it will prevent you from using that great direct marketing approach that worked so well in the US.

Danish meetings

Some Americans turn meetings into mini performances, in which they deliver a dazzling presentation that will enhance their position in the company and ultimately boost their careers.

Danes don't think of meetings the same way. Sure, they're interested in learning from a knowledgeable source, but they're expecting to be informed, not impressed.

Seeking consensus

Like many other aspects of Danish life, meetings are an equitable affair where everyone down to the student worker is expected to share information and then have his or her say, and in a best-case scenario consensus can be reached.

Sometimes this consensus-seeking goes on for far too long, resulting in a snap decision by the boss, who just can't take it any more.

No written agenda

Danish meetings don't always have a written agenda, but they usually have a declared purpose, and it's a good idea to be prepared before you go in.

The quickest way to lose a Dane's respect is to waste their time.

Sadly, some Danish meetings will waste your time, as they meander about and wander off into side alleys.

Assuming that the meeting has a set endpoint, it's OK to get up at that time and claim another engagement.

Meeting refreshments

It's common to have a bowl of sweets at a Danish meeting; despite their glowing good health, Danes are among the world's top consumers of candy.

When external customers are present, this is sometimes upgraded to cake or a fruit plate.

Everyone pours their own coffee in a Danish meeting, and usually tidies up their own dishes afterwards.

Language concerns

As a non-Danish speaker, your presence will mean the meeting must be held in English.

This is usually not a problem for younger members of the team, but some older staff may feel a little shy in English.

Often these older employees have important product or customer knowledge. Yet they may be reluctant to make points and pose questions in front of the group because they're not confident of their language abilities.

You can counteract this by asking specifically for their opinion, or by taking them aside later one-to-one and asking if they have any concerns.

When to schedule a meeting

In Danish families with young children, one parent generally drops off the kids at school or the local day care center, while the other picks up the kids at the end of the day.

If you are so foolish as to schedule a meeting before 9am or after 3pm, you risk upsetting this family system.

The parents will have to switch places, or one parent will have to do both drop-off and pick-up, and everyone will be in a sour mood.

Avoid headaches by scheduling your meetings between 9:30am and 2:30pm.

If you insist on planning a meeting outside those hours, people will be there if they have to be, but they won't be happy about it.

Don't say "Let's have lunch" unless you mean it

Maybe you're just being your usual outgoing self, chatting with a Danish contact or business partner, and a big event in your life comes up in conversation.

You could be going through a divorce or a complex fertility process, or perhaps a family member has been involved in a crime and is struggling with the court system.

Whatever it is, it's close to your heart and you can't help talking about it, sometimes in depth, in that open-hearted way familiar to viewers of afternoon talk shows.

Danes usually don't talk about such intimate things with people they don't know well. So when you do, they immediately think *Now we are friends.*

Friendship is a deep relationship

For Danes, friendship is a deep and often lifelong relationship. It means you can rely on each other through thick and thin.

From your point of view, you were just getting something off your chest, but from their point of view, sharing such intimate experiences is a form of commitment.

When it doesn't turn out that way, there are hurt feelings and sometimes a bit of anger that Americans are so flaky and superficial.

Danes don't understand fuzzy promises

This is also true of more casual statements. "Let's have lunch sometime," you may say to someone just to get them off the phone or put an end to an overlong chat.

It never occurs to your Danish contact that you have only a flimsy intent of actually having lunch with him.

The same is true for other statements of intent, like "Let's get together for a beer" or "We should definitely go for a run around the lakes at some point."

Danes are quite literal-minded and don't understand the fuzzy nature of these promises. They will be looking forward to the beer or the run around the lakes and rather hurt when it never comes to pass.

Alternately, they may say quite bluntly, "Thanks, but I

really don't have time to go for a run with you."

That may sound rude to you, but to your Danish contact, honesty and directness are better than airy promises that will never be fulfilled.

What Danes think of Americans

Generally Danes like Americans, and Americans like to be liked, which is a good basis for business and business relationships. Danes see Americans as friendly, open, and positive.

That said, the Danish media feeds its readers a steady diet of all the most shocking things that 350 million Americans can come up with, with a special emphasis on anything that feeds pre-existing prejudices about obesity, guns, and social discord.

The "Bible Belt" appears frequently in Danish media as the sort of thing its readers should look down upon.

Big brother must be cut down to size

Denmark is a small country, so it's not always evident to your Danish business contact that something going on in rural Oregon doesn't entirely reflect your experiences in suburban Wisconsin or vice-versa.

And when Danes talk about the US, the Danish anti-authoritarian streak is often visible. "Big Brother" countries must be constantly cut down to size.

Danes have a similar relationship to Sweden, and the Danish media take a peculiar glee in reporting anything going wrong there.

American culture is popular

Danes do like American culture, in particular American music.

In Jylland, the part of Denmark with the most farms and agriculture, US country music is popular. There are even square-dancing clubs.

US gospel music is popular all over Denmark; several small cities have their own gospel choirs. It's inspiring to see large groups of Danes embracing music that is part of the cultural heritage of Black America.

Many Danes also like to follow American sports, particularly basketball and NFL football.

Baseball, on the other hand, looks a lot like the Danish children's game of roundball, and to see big strong men playing it for money looks to them like a professional league for Duck Duck Goose.

Thoughts on American food

American food consumption habits are likely to come up in conversation. McDonald's is big in Denmark, and some Danes seem convinced that Americans eat nothing else.

If you're welcoming Danish business contacts to the US, try introducing them to Kansas City BBQ, New England crab cakes, California Asian fusion cuisine, New Orleans gumbo, or some excellent TexMex.

There are a few TexMex restaurants in Denmark, but quality is often lacking. I never had a brown Margarita until one was served to me in Denmark.

When Denmark is in the media

Being citizens of a petite country that plays a minor role on the world stage, Danes are thrilled whenever they are mentioned in the international media.

Their European football championship in 1992 is something they love to discuss – they beat Germany, another big brother country! – and so is a visit by Oprah to Denmark in 2009. (She stopped by one of the most expensive apartments in Copenhagen and marveled at the huge windows and fabulous view from this "typical Danish home.")

If a story about Denmark appears on any major US website or TV channel while you are doing business with the Danes, they may ask if you have seen it and then launch into an explanation of how the American reporter got it wrong.

Know your famous Danes

It's also not a bad idea to do a Google search for "World's Most Famous Danes" before you head out for a social occasion with your Danish colleagues.

They are very proud of the athletes, actors, and musicians on this ever-changing list, and they will be impressed and somewhat touched that you know who they are.

Small talk with Danes

Americans sometimes find silence uncomfortable. When conversation flags, they often try to fill up the empty space with random chatter, stilted laughter, or in a worst-case scenario, whistling and humming.

Danes, like most Northern Europeans, don't feel this way. They are comfortable with silence.

What they find stressful is small talk.

Automating it away

Having to make small talk is so intimidating that one of my customers, an engineering firm, asked if they might be able to automate it in their emails to their American colleagues.

They suggested a program that would scrape their colleagues' local weather report – "I hear you're having a lot of rain over there!" and sports reports, "Tough loss in the fourth quarter!" – and automatically insert them into the opening lines of the email, leaving the engineers to focus on actual business.

Don't say "How are you?"

In particular, Danes hate the question *How are you?*

They don't know how to answer it, and sometimes get frustrated with their American colleague who asks the question and then doesn't have the patience to listen to an in-depth answer.

I recommend avoiding *How are you?* entirely.

Either pare it down to a slim *Good to see you!* or flip it to a quick yes-or-no question like "Did you get out and enjoy the good weather this weekend?" Alternately, prepare a more detailed question related to the person's business role.

Small talk with Danes

If you're invited to a Danish dinner party or company holiday party, you'll find yourself in a situation where you need to make small talk with Danes for hours.

Most dinner parties are set up at long tables where you'll be fixed in place, leaving you with the option of talking to the person on your right, the person on your left, and occasionally the people across the table from you, depending on the noise level.

Reliable topics include travel (the Danes love to go places during their annual five weeks of vacation), gardening and home renovation, amateur sports clubs they may be involved with, and all of the ways Denmark is better than the United States – a topic the Danes never tire of.

If you enjoy talking US politics, the Danes will too, although you'll enjoy this more if you are a Democrat than if you are a Republican.

Topics to steer clear of

Topics to steer clear of include personal finance and salaries, the Danish Royal Family (many people adore them, others call them "Denmark's biggest welfare recipients"), and anything that would make you appear to be bragging about your own family's accomplishments.

There's also no need to expound on whether or not you have Danish ancestry if it goes any further back than your own parents.

The Danes will politely nod at your connections to the Danish ethnic family, but they will find it about as interesting as you would find the discovery of a previously unknown second cousin once removed.

Danish patriotism

I once heard a man say that no country in the world displayed its flag as much as the Americans did.

That man had clearly not been to Denmark, where the Danish flag appears on cakes, Christmas trees, and even plastic cucumber wrapping.

The Danes love their flag, which is the oldest in the world in continuous use and the model for similar flags used by Sweden, Norway, Finland, and Iceland.

Danish flags and birthdays

In particular, the Danish flag is associated with birthdays. Should your birthday come around while you are in Denmark, your colleagues may put a cloth Danish flag on a little brass flagpole in your workspace or by your plate at lunch.

This isn't a political symbol. It just means "joy."

When members of the Danish Royal Family have birthdays, tiny cloth flags are attached to many of the local buses.

It's a national sport to figure out who is being celebrated, often someone who is entirely forgotten for the rest of the year.

Danes love their Constitution

The Danes are as fond of their Constitution as the Americans are, and it is frequently cited whenever a legal dispute is in the news.

Constitution Day is celebrated with a half-day off every June 5, and people accused of a crime in Denmark are taken to court for a "constitutional hearing."

When I became a Danish citizen, I was sent in the mail a small paperback version of the Danish constitution.

While admirable, it is also complex and wordy, lacking the simple poetry of the US Bill of Rights. I must admit I never read it all the way through.

The Danish military

The Danish military is small – only about 12,000 active-duty personnel – and co-operates extensively with the US military. Danish Air Force pilots are trained in Texas, for example.

Denmark still has a military draft. Every man turning 18 gets a number that may or may not be called up, and there are usually not enough spots for everyone who would like to serve.

Being a soldier or a sailor in Denmark doesn't generate the automatic respect sometimes given to members of the US military.

That said, the Royal Life Guards, which guard the Royal Family, are an extremely high-status group.

In addition to general army training, the Life Guards stand long hours wearing tall bearskin hats outside the various palaces, protecting the royalty inside.

The Life Guards are where the future titans of Denmark meet each other, and saying their child is a member of *Livgarden* is one of the few things Danish parents dare to brag about.

Design in Denmark

Design is a passion in Denmark, particularly interior design, which makes perfect sense in a culture where people spend so much time in their homes during the long, dark winter.

Danish design furniture, with its simple, elegant lines, is popular (and widely counterfeited) all over the world.

Utility and grace in every setting

Even outside the home, you'll notice that things in Denmark are carefully set up to flow with maximum utility and grace, from the beautiful new circular line of the Copenhagen metro to the sleek new bicycle bridge across Odense Harbor, to the circular rainbow walk atop the Aarhus art museum to the curvy, streamlined toilets found in every public restroom.

I even notice the difference when I fill out my tax forms, which I have the privilege of doing for both the Danish tax authorities and the IRS.

The American forms look like they were designed by a yawning bureaucrat using fifteen-year-old software.

The Danish tax forms are clear, concise, and gorgeous – although the tax rates are also much more ambitious.

Make design a priority

What this means in business terms is that whatever you produce or deliver in Denmark, whether it is a product or promotional materials, must be beautifully designed, preferably by a Dane.

American style can look boxy and obvious to Danish eyes.

Don't ever give your Danish business partners something put together by an amateur, or anything printed on shoddy paper or made with cheap materials.

In the Danish market a low price is welcome, but quality and polish are much more important.

Working for a Danish boss

Interviewing for a job in Denmark and working with a Danish team are topics I've covered in more detail in my previous book, *How to Work in Denmark*.

Here, however, are a few general rules about working for a Danish boss.

Independence vs inspiration

Being a boss is a funny kind of position in Denmark, a thoroughly anti-authoritarian culture.

Bosses are breaking one of the first rules of Denmark by being, in fact, in authority over others, so they tend to compensate by not being too domineering.

This means Danish bosses provide much more independence and much less guidance and inspiration than you are accustomed to in the US.

Ask your Danish boss how you should tackle a problem and she may say, "*Well, how do you think you should handle it?*"

Fewer specific instructions

Expect much less in the way of specific instructions and much more discussion of process and how to reach a consensus.

Indirect orders are common. "I think it would be useful to have this done by Friday," means, in fact, that it should be done by Friday. Ask if you're not sure.

Bosses in Denmark also don't need to pretend they're all-seeing or all-knowing, as US bosses sometimes do.

"I'm not sure – ask someone on my team," is a perfectly reasonable thing for a Danish boss to say.

More trust, less monitoring

You will not be monitored as much in Denmark and you will be trusted more, but that trust is something that you must treat as precious.

Calling in sick when you're not really sick is not done in Denmark. Take a "personal day" instead.

And never say you understand a concept when you really don't quite get it, or insist you've got a situation under control when you really haven't.

These are behaviors that will destroy a Danish boss's trust in you.

Boss for now, not forever

Jobs in Denmark are almost never lifetime appointments, so one of the most important things you can get from your employer is continuing education in your field.

At the annual "employee conversation," make sure to come equipped with a few suggestions for courses or conferences that will serve both the company's interests and your own.

These events will make sure that your knowledge is up-to-date and help you fill up your LinkedIn connections (Danes love LinkedIn) with the sort of contacts in your industry that will help you get your next job with your next Danish boss.

The visitor who wasn't equal

An American businesswoman made a big mistake while visiting her company's Danish office.

She flew into the local airport, rented a car, drove to the office, and met with the top person there.

Then she got back in the car, drove back to the airport, and flew away.

Meeting just with the top person – and not taking the time to greet the rest of the people in the office – was a crime against equality.

Shake everyone's hand

The correct thing to do would have been to schedule enough time in Denmark to go through the office and meet every person on the team, at the very least for a quick handshake and a few moments of business-related conversation.

Even better would have been scheduling enough time to join the group lunch that is common in Danish offices.

Even better than that would have been a few "get to know you" meetings with the various teams and team leaders to show that she was interested in their projects and was aware of their concerns.

Don't drop by

In fact, the only thing the visitor did right was to schedule her visit well in advance and send a detailed agenda so that the person she was meeting could be fully prepared.

Danes are not spontaneous people, in either their professional or social lives. It is common for them to make plans months ahead.

Never "drop in" on a Dane unexpectedly. On the other hand, if you accept an invitation, don't cancel unless you are ill.

If a Dane has put aside time for you, he has offered you a bit of his most valuable resource.

Assume everyone is useful

There is little dead wood in Danish companies. People are simply too expensive, and the termination process too straightforward, particularly if layoffs are done in groups or buyouts are offered.

Reliably assume that everyone you meet has a useful role, regardless of their title, since Danes generally don't care that much about titles anyway.

This includes student workers, usually college or graduate students who are invited to meetings. The company hopes to hire the best ones for full-time jobs as soon as they are available.

Be kind to the piccoline

In fact, the only people not included in meetings are the office handyman and the *piccolo* or *piccoline*, usually a very young person hired to clean up the kitchen and occasionally act as receptionist.

That said, these people should also be treated with respect and never with irritation, no matter how busy or frustrated you might be with your schedule or travel arrangements or your inability to type in the wireless password.

If you snap at somebody in a Danish office, everyone will hear about it, and your reputation will not be enhanced.

Negotiating with Danes

Danes have a great love of transparency – which they see as an element of one of their other great loves, authenticity – and this is reflected in their negotiation style.

They're not there to play 4D chess or create drama at peak moments.

They're there to get a deal done that can potentially build a long-term relationship based on openness and trust.

Extreme transparency

Sometimes the Danes can be so transparent that it seems a little comic.

An acquaintance told me how she was chatting with a Danish business associate before an upcoming negotiation.

"What's your top bid?" she asked him.

"Fifty," said her associate.

"What's your opening bid?"

"Fifty," he replied.

Co-operation in a small country

That doesn't mean the Danes are suckers. With centuries of merchant tradition behind them, they enjoy a good business deal.

In particular, people from Jylland are known for being tough negotiators.

But like so many things in Denmark, the negotiation approach is based on co-operation instead of confrontation.

It's important to remember that Denmark is a small country and everyone knows everyone, specifically within industries.

If you're found to be a cheat, overly dramatic, or an unreliable partner, word will get around quickly.

Simple, practical agreements

Denmark is a much less litigious society than the US, so your Danish partner will assume a handshake deal is valid long before the written contracts arrive.

Alternately, your partner will outline the points of your agreement in an email and ask you to reply "OK" if you agree. This serves as a quick 'n' dirty written contract.

It's important to know, however, the Danes have an extremely flexible and practical approach to business.

When market conditions change, they will often try to adjust agreements to match.

The Danish way of customer service

In a large, highly competitive market like the US, you often do cartwheels to keep your customer happy.

This is less true in Denmark, a small market that is somewhat protected by the limited number of people who speak Danish.

In Denmark, the needs of a company's employees are often considered equal to if not more important than the needs of its customers.

For example, on Christmas Eve, the buses in many Danish cities stop running from 5pm until 11pm so the bus drivers can eat Christmas Eve dinner with their families.

Bus riders who want to eat dinner with *their* families should plan to arrive by 4pm and stay until midnight.

No "go above and beyond"

Danish customers haven't been conditioned to expect all the go-above-and-beyond and extra freebies that American customers often demand.

A bad night in a hotel with the fire alarm going off by accident twice won't get you a free stay; a request for water while dining in a restaurant will result in the server opening an expensive bottle.

An acquaintance leased an expensive luxury car and, as he was leaving the showroom, asked for a plastic phone holder for the dashboard. He was charged $15 for it.

Internationals living in Denmark constantly complain about bad customer service and, if they are nonwhite, sometimes see it as racially motivated. Racism does exist in Denmark, but lousy customer service is widely available to all.

Danes repatriating from the US usually say that American customer service is what they miss most.

A good product sells itself

In Danish shops, salespeople are sometimes lackadaisical or invisible.

A business contact of mine opened a little shop selling high-end Danish souvenirs – Danish whisky, Danish honey, Danish art posters – but after a trial period, stopped hiring Danish personnel in favor of internationals only.

She said her inventory required storytelling and introduction – *"This honey was collected from a hive on top of Copenhagen City Hall"* – and the Danish hires didn't feel comfortable doing that.

Shouldn't a good product sell itself? they thought, while hanging out around the cash register.

Nobody wanted to be pushy.

Crime and punishment

Denmark is a low-crime society, but it is not a no-crime society.

Your smartphone or laptop will disappear quickly if left in the wrong place, bicycle theft is common, and the country has the unhappy position of being Europe's number-one spot for home burglaries. Thieves just can't resist those great Danish design housewares.

That said, penalties are not as draconian as they sometimes are in the US. Many prisons work on the "open plan" where convicted individuals can come and go to work, school and other approved activities while serving their sentence.

Since everyone in Denmark has to register their home

address with the state and use a government-provided number for the health and banking systems, it's hard to run away and hide for very long.

A big, fat fine

Instead of prison, what the Danes really love is a fine – a big, fat fine.

Caught speeding in your car? That will be $600. Bicyclists can be fined too: $100 for riding on the sidewalk, $200 for running a red light, or $300 for biking while intoxicated.

Fines are also imposed if you ride the bus, metro, or train without precisely the right ticket.

The roving "controllers" are merciless professionals who won't buy your claim of being a confused foreigner and will sometimes take you off the train to discuss payment.

Most Danes have stories about getting caught by the controllers themselves.

Pay your taxes

The crime that you really must be sure not to commit, however, is tax evasion.

The Danish social welfare system relies on everyone paying their share, and people or companies who are revealed to be cheaters will find their reputations in tatters.

Fortunately, the Danish tax department is somewhat

more accessible and interactive than the IRS.

You or your accountant can call and chat about precisely how big your tax should be.

Danish humor and conflict avoidance

Humor and aggression are mixed up with each other in Denmark, a conflict-adverse society that can use a joke either to lighten the mood or deliver a withering put-down – and it can be hard to tell which is which.

Danes use sarcasm so frequently that they sometimes forget they're doing it.

And they rarely smile at their own joke, or add a disclaimer like "Just kidding." Instead, the statement simply hangs in the air.

Was it funny? Was it nasty? Was it both?

Combined with some Americans' eagerness to be offended, this toxic brew can eat away at cross-cultural teamwork.

Equality and Danish humor

Danish humor has its roots in the country's passion for equality: everyone, no matter how high or how low, is expected to be able to make fun of themselves.

Being able to take a joke – to not take yourself too seriously – is an important part of being considered a good person in Denmark.

And unlike Americans, who make fun of situations, Danes go directly to making fun of *people*.

If you mention, for example, that the breakfast in your hotel was sub-par, some witty colleague might say, "Well, you're American. You ought to be used to bad food."

The joy of human imperfectability

Cutting remarks can also be used to discipline people who step out of line, or to cut someone down to size if they break the diktats of equality.

But Danish humor can also joyfully celebrate human imperfectability, as it does with the "failure beer" (*kvajebajer*) or, during working hours, the "failure cake."

When you've made an avoidable mistake, the Danish way is to admit it and buy a beer for everyone who has seen you fumble, or offer the team an afternoon cake. Cake brings people together in Denmark.

For Americans, admitting you were wrong can be

difficult, in part because you don't want to lose your air of authority, and in part because you don't want to get sued.

It's more tempting to try to cover your backside or blame someone else.

But owning up to your fumbles and missteps can go a long way towards earning you the respect of your Danish team.

Denmark is not just Copenhagen

One of the things that surprised me when I first moved to Denmark is that there could be so many distinctions and divisions between fewer than six million people living in an area half the size of Indiana.

But the differences exist, and they are deeply felt.

Stopping by Copenhagen and saying you've seen Denmark is a little bit like stopping by Manhattan and Disney World and saying you've seen the United States. (And many Danes do precisely this.)

Dry humor in Jylland

While Copenhagen is both the capital of the country and its business center, much of the country's wealth is generated in Jylland, the large land mass stuck to Germany.

Jylland is the source of most of Denmark's agricultural exports, particularly pork, and many of its best engineers, who these days largely concern themselves with green energy technology.

People from Jylland are known for their extremely dry humor and low excitement levels, which become more pronounced the further north you go.

I found this out for myself when I brought my "How to Live in Denmark Game Show" comedy presentation to Brande, a town of about 7000 out in the countryside. The same jokes that had wowed audiences numerous times elsewhere in the country earned only stone-faced silence, and the occasional upturned mouth corner.

After it was over, I apologized to the organizer, and said I was sorry that they hadn't liked the show.

"What do you mean?" she said. "They had a great time."

"This is how they look when they're having a great time."

Different regional accents

Danes from various parts of Denmark also have sharply different accents. Some regional dialects, like *Bornholmsk* and *Sønderjysk*, are so specialized that people speaking them are subtitled on Danish TV.

It's common for urban types to make fun of people who speak like they come from the countryside, calling them *bonderøv*, or "farmer butts."

The "proper" dialect-free version of Danish is *rigsdansk* – Danish as spoken by the monarch. In addition, there is a government agency that updates the dictionary, approves spellings, and produces complex rules about commas that have even highly educated Danes tearing their hair out.

On a daily basis, most Danes speak a casual, urban form of the language, peppered with English words and a good deal of English-language profanity.

Many think these words are fun and colorful and have no idea why anyone might be offended by them.

Drive the Daisy Route

If you have a good amount of time in Denmark and are itching to get behind the wheel of a car, consider taking a short trip along *The Marguerite Route*, otherwise known as the Daisy Route, a 2200-mile network of small roads through the prettiest parts of the Danish countryside.

You'll see the magnificent white-sand beaches of West Jylland, the straw-roofed houses in villages on Fyn, the treacherous chalk cliffs at Møns, and the beautiful castle at Helsingør that features in Shakespeare's "Hamlet."

Taking a weekend off to explore the Danish countryside will give you a sense of the natural diversity of this green, peaceful country, something you can't fully appreciate in the taxi between your office and the airport.

Driving in Denmark

While a car is useful for exploring the Danish countryside, a car in one of Denmark's larger cities can be a millstone around your neck.

The traffic is terrible, the fuel costs stratospheric, the parking spaces doll-sized. Bicyclists own the road and often ignore traffic rules.

Even if the company you're visiting is in the suburbs or exurbs, there's a good chance you'll save money by taking a cab – and most Danish taxis are Mercedes-Benz or Teslas. (There is no Uber or Lyft in Denmark.)

Watch out for bicyclists

If you do choose to drive in the city, be very careful about right turns. Several Danish bicyclists are killed every year because a car or truck took a right turn and the bicyclist (who may be drunk, on his phone, or simply not paying attention) continued going straight.

There is no legal right turn on red in Denmark, and even on green, the bicyclist has the right of way.

You might choose to bike to work yourself, which is common in Denmark, even for executives. Many offices contain showers so commuters can clean up and change into their business gear.

If you do bike, don't dawdle in the bike lanes – these people are commuters, this is rush hour, and they don't want a gawking tourist clogging up their passing lane.

150% tax on new cars

Denmark has never had a car industry, which is why the government is able to get away with such high car taxes – 85% to 150% of the purchase price of a new vehicle – and why many Danish cities actively discourage car traffic.

Most Danes are good drivers, although they have a weird fondness for U-turns at unexpected moments.

While the Danes are hearty drinkers, the penalties for driving while intoxicated are substantial.

A blood alcohol level above 0.5% will get you in trouble, so if you've had more than a single glass of wine or beer, call a cab.

Dining with the Danes

Unlike the Norwegians, Swedes, and some Germans, the Danes don't show their cultural pride by dressing up in 19th century folklore outfits. (The first time I ever saw a Danish version was at a Danish culture festival in Solvang, California.)

Instead, Danes express their cultural pride through food.

When visiting Denmark, you'll be offered Danish cuisine, and expressing enthusiasm for it will go a long way towards generating harmony with your Danish colleagues.

Vegans and carnivores

Danish cuisine has something for everyone. If you're a carnivore, don't miss the Danish pork dishes, particularly *flæskesteg*, the crispy, fatty fried pork that's the official national food.

For people who prefer fish, there's a great selection in this country surrounded by water. Curried herring and fried plaice are popular, and so are many types of salmon. I like the thinly-sliced smoked salmon served on rye bread with chives, dill, and a bit of chopped red onion.

Vegans can enjoy a great selection of root vegetables, wonderful fresh Danish berries, or the sweet elderflower juice that is sometimes blended with vodka or champagne.

Denmark's famous thick bread, *rugbrød*, is vegan-friendly and can be eaten with potatoes on top as a type of *smørrebrød*, the open-faced sandwiches that are popular at lunchtime.

Sweet tastes

Danes adore cake and candy, in particular salt licorice, which is a national passion.

Make room in your food plan for a real Danish pastry, which are nothing like the ones you get in a plastic bag from the vending machine at home. Made daily with fresh cream and the famous Danish butter, they are worth every calorie.

There's also an old-fashioned dessert called *rødgrød med fløde*, a kind of berry porridge. I've never been served this dish in real life, but Danes think it's hilarious to try to make foreigners pronounce it.

At a restaurant

Much of your dining with the Danes will probably be lunches at corporate canteens, which all but the very smallest employers provide for their employees.

"Going out for lunch" is rare in Denmark, and some smaller towns may not even have restaurants open at this time of day.

A weekday breakfast at a restaurant is very unusual, although weekend brunch is popular in the big cities.

At any time of day, your restaurant experience will be different in Denmark than in the US, because Denmark has no cheap labor or tipping culture.

Employees are highly paid and there are fewer of them. In many cafés, you'll order at the bar, pay in advance, and then pick up your own food when it's ready.

If you do have a server, they will not be particularly attentive – no refills! – and the chef won't be accustomed to making changes to the menu based on your allergies or dietary preferences.

Most restaurant kitchens close at 9pm, and unless the place is also a bar, you're expected to be out the door by 10pm.

Tipping is not required, although you can always slightly "round up," paying DK200 for a DK185 bill, for example.

Don't rush home

In the US, dining out is often part of a longer evening. You go to dinner and a movie, or dinner and out for drinks and dancing afterwards.

In Denmark, the dinner is the evening.

Whether dining at a business contact's home or in a restaurant, you are expected to sit in one chair for many hours, conversing with the people on both sides of you and polishing off multiple bottles of wine or beer.

When I first arrived in Denmark, I unintentionally offended many people by leaving too early.

I was thinking from the American point of view: I didn't want to stay too long and make myself a nuisance.

That's not how the Danes think. Long evenings are something you will have to get used to, along with some Danes' disconcerting habit of eating a hamburger with a knife and fork.

Avoid cheerful hot air

Americans love inspirational items.

Whether it's a poster that says "Today is a good day to realize how far you've come" or a notepad that says "Storms don't last forever" or even a book called "100 Pep Talks" (all of which I recently found in a single store in Atlanta's Ponce City Market), there's always a market for slogans that provide encouragement for life in a competitive society.

Danes don't do this kind of optimistic self-help. They are ruthlessly practical people who think in precise, factual terms.

We're number one!
Some American bosses like to energize their teams with chanting similar to a political or sports rally: *"We're number one!" "We can do it!" "We will win!"* or other uplifting slogans.

This will have your Danish employees rolling their eyes.

According to which parameters are we number one? they might ask. *And why is being number one useful when it comes to achieving our corporate mission and vision, serving our customers, and creating a better workplace?*

If you try to pump up your team with cheerful hot air, they will think you are silly.

Mindfulness yes, astrology no

In general, appeals to the inspirational or spiritual side of life fall flat for the Danes, who are nominally Christian but in practice go to church only for baptisms, confirmations, weddings, and funerals.

While mindfulness and meditation are popular as stress relievers, new-age religions like astrology, crystals, and psychics are seen as odd or immature.

Don't ask your new Danish colleague what his sun sign is and then predict you'll work together harmoniously.

The only exception is numerology, perhaps because Danes are so deeply proud of their names.

I know of more than one Danish woman who has changed her name in mid-life in order to change her luck, based on what her numerologist recommended.

Health care and the Danish social welfare system

When visiting the US recently, I stopped in a diner for breakfast and ordered eggs and toast.

"What type of bread would you like for your toast?" the server asked. "We have white, wheat, rye, sourdough, pumpernickel, cinnamon raisin, and bagels."

The overwhelming toast selection is a rough metaphor for the US health system: so many options it can be overwhelming, along with labyrinthine insurance systems and ludicrous billing.

There are no diners in Denmark, but if you go to a restaurant, they will offer you one type of bread.

Tax-funded, with fewer choices

This corresponds to the Danish public health system. It

is tax-funded and you will rarely have to fill out a form, but you will have fewer choices.

The state will tell you what you are eligible for and when you are eligible to receive it. Urgent care is delivered efficiently, but for non-urgent care you may have to wait a bit.

This is why millions of Danes pay for additional private insurance, and it is a staple of corporate recruitment packages.

And while *over treatment* is a problem in the US – along with "defensive medicine" and too many tests – *under treatment* is common in Denmark.

Don't be surprised if you're told to take the equivalent of a Tylenol and a nap for everything from knee pain to recovery from a C-section.

Social welfare is popular

Danes love their cradle-to-grave welfare state. In two decades of living here, I've never met a single person who wanted it dismantled.

But it is a commitment, a national commitment. Everyone with the ability to work *must* work, and must pay substantial taxes, in order to finance the services shared by all.

At the same time, everyone accepts that there will be

limits on services so there are enough to go around.

For example, many expensive new drugs are simply not offered in Denmark, even if they could save the lives of individual patients.

There's only so much money that can be spent on health, and in the Danish system, it must be distributed as equally as possible.

What it means to you

The Danes use the word "welfare" to cover not just direct income transfers, but universal health, unemployment compensation, and tax-financed education.

To keep everyone honest, the system is sometimes an iron fist in a velvet glove.

So while unemployment payments are generous – up to 90% of your working income for as long as two years – receiving them requires regular visits with a personal job counselor and proof that you are actively looking for work.

This may drive you crazy if you are a hiring manager, since you will receive half-hearted applications from people who are sending them only to satisfy their job counselor.

Homelessness and basic income

Even if they can't (or won't) find work, very few people are down and out in Denmark: homelessness is much less common than it is in the USA.

Danes who have exhausted every other resource can get a small basic income, although they are required to sell non-essential assets like jewelry and motorcycles before they are eligible.

Only legal residents of Denmark can receive this assistance, and many Danish homeless shelters accept legal residents only. If you see someone sleeping rough, they are likely to be a migrant.

Begging is illegal in Denmark – police do make arrests – and unauthorized encampments in urban areas are illegal too. Danish police quickly clear these camps away.

You'll often see migrants collecting cans and bottles in order to redeem the deposit at local supermarkets.

If you're drinking beer in a park (which is allowed in Denmark) collectors may ask if you're finished with your bottle so they can take it and exchange it for cash.

Some things you don't get

Many Americans who are fans of the Danish social welfare system assume if offers everything they get in the US, plus more.

They usually miss the half of the equation in which they will also have to *give* much more in taxes, plus accept limits on what they receive.

For example, Danish universities are tax-funded, so

students pay no tuition and even receive a small stipend to live on while they study.

But there are limited spaces in many of the popular subjects, such as journalism and dentistry.

If you don't get one of those slots, you'll have to rethink your life choices, or study abroad and miss building up the local network that is so important to career success.

The "happiest country in the world"

When I hear that Denmark is the "happiest country in the world," I'm skeptical, but I do believe Danes have fewer daily worries because of their social welfare system.

Plenty of individuals manage to manufacture their own unhappiness by cheating on their partners, drinking too much alcohol, living beyond their means, and other classic vices.

When there are no foreigners around, Danes have plenty of complaints (or *brok*, which rhymes with "clock") about the lapses and blunders of their social welfare system.

(One classic joke: "*We don't have capital punishment in Denmark. Instead, we have the public health service.*")

But to the outside world, they will defend it as passionately as they defend the Danish flag.

Diversity and the Danes

In southern Florida, "Manatee mailboxes" are popular. To show your support for conserving local wildlife, you can order a five-foot-tall fiberglass version of this dolphin-like animal to cradle your mailbox in its fins.

It's crazy and fun and a little bit weird – and it's utterly unthinkable in Denmark, where practicality and modesty are the order of the day.

Being different just for the sheer whimsy of it is not the Danish way.

One American mother told me of collecting her daughter from the government day care center only to find that all her colorful hair ribbons had been taken out.

"It made her look too different from the other children," the day care worker said.

Danish with an accent

Although Copenhagen, Aarhus, Esbjerg, and Odense have been trading cities for centuries and are accustomed to a wide range of humans, much of Denmark is still a series of villages where people have lived for centuries.

Outsiders are always a little suspect. Even Danes who move from one part of Denmark to another say it can be almost impossible to make friends.

And while you're probably accustomed to hearing English spoken in many different ways, Danes are not used to hearing Danish spoken with a foreign accent.

Almost every international who has taken pains to learn Danish has a story about their pronunciation being mocked and laughed at, along with suggestions that they should just give up trying to learn Danish.

Personally, I was told that my accent made it impossible to understand my order for a hot dog at a local sausage wagon.

Ethnic diversity

Denmark is no longer the all-white country it was 50 years ago.

People of color can be found at every level of the economic

spectrum: high-income specialists recruited by Denmark's biggest companies; middle-class people married to Danes; and less well-off refugees and their descendants, who often live in poor neighborhoods the Danish government insists on officially labelling as "ghettos."

Whatever their origin or income class, newcomers are expected to conform to Danish culture and contribute to the welfare state by working and paying taxes.

People who can do this are generally welcome, and people who can't are not.

The Danish government goes so far as to release statistics that show whether newcomers from specific countries are an economic plus or minus for Denmark. (US immigrants are in the "plus" category, as are newcomers from China and India, who are often skilled IT professionals.)

Most of the top levels of Danish politics and business are still populated by ethnic Danes, who make up 87% of the population.

There are, however, a few prominent politicians of diverse backgrounds. As younger generations move into the Danish workplace, there will probably be more diversity in positions of power.

What to wear in Denmark

Danish fashion is applauded in all the major style outlets, which cover the fabulous runway shows at Copenhagen Fashion Week.

In real life, though, Danes are not flashy dressers. They wear simple, dark clothing designed for the unpredictable Danish weather. Designer labels are seen as a little tacky for anyone past their teenage years. Quality is more important than trends.

And while it's a standard American opening remark to compliment someone's cool jacket or cute earrings, Danes will think it's odd if you comment on what they're wearing.

Basic business casual

A basic business casual wardrobe will take you through most of your appointments in Denmark. Blazer, sweater, shirt and trousers – all in subtle colors – and you're ready to go.

This outfit will make you look equal to the rest of your team, and equality is an essential part of Danish culture.

Anti-authoritarian dressing

A business contact recently told me about a young American woman visiting Denmark to make a presentation.

Eager to present herself as a powerful figure, she wore a chic suit and the highest heels she could manage.

It was the wrong signal. First of all, high heels are uncommon in Denmark; too much walking is required, and cobblestone streets don't play well with heels.

Secondly, the anti-authoritarian Danes don't like people who act or look like they're better than anyone else.

A simple outfit in fine fabrics, perhaps with a piece of statement jewelry, would have made a much better impression.

Don't be sloppy

There are also Americans who go too far in the other direction, showing up for work in sweatpants, surfer shorts, and shower shoes, or with their wet hair covered by a baseball cap.

This won't do. The Danes will think you are childish and unreliable.

Danes also don't share the American passion for sunglasses, in part because Denmark is grey and rainy for much of the year.

If for some reason you don't want to look American, put away your shades – and smile less often.

Gifts in Denmark

It is never necessary to bring a gift as part of doing business in Denmark. In fact, it may make your counterpart uncomfortable, since most companies have strict limits on what their employees can accept.

However, if you're invited to a private home in Denmark for dinner, it can be nice to bring a thoughtful gift for the host or hostess.

Specialty foods from your region

Specialty foods from your area of the US are always a hit: maple syrup, hot sauce, micro-brewed beer, local candy (but not chocolate: US chocolate is seen as deeply inferior to the European version.)

Don't bring fruit, cheeses, or meats, which you might not be able to get past customs.

No gag gifts or knick-knacks

Avoid gag gifts (*One can of pure New York City air!*) and knick-knacks. Danish homes are small and nobody has room for any clutter.

If your host has teenage children and you'd like to bring them a gift too, a jersey from your local sports team is usually welcome.

Danes and English

Danish children start learning English in school when they're six years old, and many pick up a few words and phrases in English before that through online videos and music.

That means that the majority of your Danish business partners will speak excellent English, with the occasional exception of older team members who came of age at a time when English was less important.

Still, they are not native speakers, and many learned from teachers who were not native speakers, so you'll still hear some occasional errors.

The most common ones have to do with irregular plurals ("My home has nice new **furnitures**") and subject-verb agreement ("**We are** very busy. **He are** very busy too.")

There's also a lot of confusion about the simple present tense versus the gerund (She **achieves** good results. She **is achieving** good results), a distinction that doesn't exist in Danish.

Direct translations

In general, however, Danes are very confident in English – sometimes too confident when it comes to directly translating their native language.

For example, it's very common for Danish colleagues to greet each other in the morning with *"Er du frisk?"*, which is a colloquial way of asking if they are ready for the day's professional challenges.

Translated directly, however, it comes out in English as "Are you fresh?", which sounds like an outtake from an anti-perspirant commercial.

UK vs US English

Danes have been taught that British English is the gold standard of the language and may insist that their corporate documents be in "UK English."

In practice, this generally means adding a "u" to color and replacing words like *realize* with *realise* along with a few grammatical doodles. (Some Danes seem to believe that there is a much greater distance between US and UK English – perhaps like the difference between Norwegian and Danish, another former colony/colonist relationship.)

If you're being hired in Denmark for something having to do with writing, they may ask if you can "write UK English." With a couple of hours of brushing up, you can.

Sorry, not sorry

In addition to having no direct translation for *please*, Danes are also much less likely to say "Excuse me" or "I'm sorry" than English speakers do.

(Danes do sometimes use the English word *sorry* for light transgressions – "I meant blueberries, not raspberries – *sorry*.")

But don't be surprised if someone pushing past you in a public place doesn't say anything at all.

In addition, Danes' flat tone and love of sarcasm can sometimes make them seem rude in English.

Learning Danish

Learning Danish is a must for people who want to make a life for themselves in Denmark, but it is not necessary for short business trips.

That said, even for short stays it can be useful to know the word for "thank you" – *tak* – plus "*hej*" (pronounced hi) to say hello and "*hej hej*" to say goodbye. You might also want to learn the word for your favorite beverage, whether it is *øl* (beer), *kaffe* (coffee) or *te* (tea.)

The beer is good in Denmark, but Danish cafés often

insist on serving hot tea and blended coffee in tall glasses that are painful to hold in your hands, at least until the beverage goes cold.

Some cultural differences just can't be explained.

Long-term stays in Denmark

Denmark is a lovely place to settle down for a while, or even permanently if you are ready to do battle with the immigration authorities.

Make sure you bring money. Denmark is an expensive place to live where you will own less stuff, but better stuff. There is no equivalent to the Dollar Store, Walmart, or Target in Denmark.

Over-the-counter medicines

Danes don't share Americans' passion for over-the-counter medicine. If you are a fan of Neosporin, NyQuil, Midol, Pepto-Bismol or Sinutab, bring some along. Generic Tylenol and Advil are easy to find in Denmark.

Pack extras of any personal care brands you can't live without. Items sent from the US (or anywhere else outside the EU) to Denmark require substantial postage plus withering customs and administration fees. Plan on at least $50 per item.

Bring lots of casual, warm, and waterproof clothing. You don't need huge polar jackets – Denmark rarely goes below 0 on the Fahrenheit scale – but halter tops and suede loafers will see very little service.

An apartment in Denmark

If you rent an apartment in Denmark, be aware that it will need to be spotless, repainted, and sometimes refloored when you return it. Take time-stamped photos on the day you move in to avoid arguments later.

Many urban apartments do not have bathtubs, only showers. In some cases, you will need to buy your own refrigerator and washer-dryer for a rental apartment.

Europe uses a different electrical current than the US, so leave your blenders, mixers, and hairdryers at home unless you want to constantly use them with a converter, which is a pain and a fire hazard.

Bedding systems are different, too; mattresses are thinner and there are no flat sheets.

Kitchen garbage disposals do not exist in Denmark. Instead, many communities have specific programs to pick up organic waste, which is carefully separated from plastic, metal, paper, and glass.

Air conditioning is unusual in Denmark, because the weather is rarely hot enough to require it. You can always open a window, but the windows have no screens.

Religious services

If you're a Christian and want to go to services during your time in Denmark, seek out an international church. Danish state churches, which are supported by a voluntary tax, are very quiet and usually poorly attended.

There are very small Jewish and Hindu communities in Denmark, and a large Muslim community. Muslims make up roughly 6% of the Danish population, and there are several new and attractive mosques financed from abroad.

Medical care in Denmark

Anyone with legal residence in Denmark is entitled to tax-financed Danish medical care. You will be asked to choose a doctor shortly after you arrive, selecting from a list of general practitioners close to your home address.

Ask your colleagues for recommendations; alternately, you may get some good tips from the many Facebook groups for internationals living in Denmark.

Dentistry for adults and many types of psychological care are not covered by the public system, so you'll have to pay for those services out of pocket if you need them.

Annual physicals are uncommon, and testing is less extensive. Mammograms start at age 50, for example, instead of age 40 as in much of the US.

In addition, some people of Asian or African descent living in Denmark have told me that ethnic Danish doctors aren't always familiar with medical conditions that are specific to people of color, such as sickle cell anaemia.

Finding a doctor who shares your ethnicity isn't always possible, particularly outside of the big cities.

You may need to get aggressive about your care, insisting on a second opinion, if you suspect that your doctor isn't giving you the right advice.

The Executive Summary: Top things to remember

Thanks for reading this far in the book. Here are a few points to remember when doing business in Denmark.

* * *

Danish culture is based on authenticity and trust. Don't BS anybody, and never promise anything you cannot deliver in full. Trust is the default – you are granted it, you don't have to earn it – but once lost, it is almost impossible to get back.

* * *

Denmark is an anti-authoritarian culture, so anyone who walks in acting like a big cheese will be resented and mocked. Your job title or place in the hierarchy isn't particularly important to your Danish team. They are practical people interested in what you can deliver.

* * *

For Danes, personal time outside work is very important. Don't expect your team to stay extra hours unless there's an urgent deadline, don't schedule meetings after 3pm, and be careful to avoid common vacation periods when you schedule product launches. When it comes to your team members, focus on the work produced, not the time served.

* * *

Danes resent micromanagement. They feel that if you've hired them to do a job, you should get out of the way and let them do it. The Danish "flat hierarchy" with fewer middle managers means you often don't have the personnel to keep constant watch on your team anyway. Keep in mind that because Denmark is less litigious than the US, some record-keeping can be unnecessary.

* * *

Danes have a great love for free speech and can be extremely direct, sometimes to the point of seeming rude. Occasionally, they will say uncomfortable things and then insist this was only an example of "Danish humor." At any rate, expect a great deal of sarcasm, and don't assume it is always negativity.

* * *

Cocooned in the welfare state, Danes may not understand

why Americans are so competitive and sometimes jumpy. Some of your Danish colleagues may seem unambitious, but that's because they have everything they want in life – a good job, a nice home, and plenty of free time. They will still be ambitious for their products and product quality.

* * *

Most Americans have been conditioned not to go around the world saying their country is the best of all possible countries, but Danes have no such reservations. They are quite proud of their culture and their system and are not particularly receptive to any kind of constructive criticism.

* * *

Denmark is a small, gentle, well-kept and very pretty country. Make sure to schedule some time away from business events to explore its beautiful beaches, wonderful museums, and tiny villages full of houses with straw roofs.

Appendix: A few notes on Danish history

Many books on business culture contain long, droning sections on a country's history, which might be exactly the kind of thing you thought you'd escape by choosing a business degree.

This is a short book, so here are some very short points about Danish history that might come up in business conversation.

* * *

The Vikings were in action from roughly 800 to 1100 AD. Clever traders and inventors who came up with the solar compass, boat keel, and other innovations having to do with their line of work, the Vikings were the first Europeans to visit North America.

Because many Vikings settled down in England after their raids, some English words are similar to words in modern Danish. The English word sky, for example, mimics *sky*, the Danish word for cloud.

* * *

Denmark once had an empire that included all of Norway, Iceland, northern Germany, and the southern half of Sweden. It shrank bit by bit over the centuries, and the final blow was a crushing defeat by the Germans in 1864.

This loss was heartbreaking to the Danes, and it is often referenced in popular culture.

It was a lesson on how to manage defeat in a graceful way, which comes in handy when Denmark competes at international sporting events.

* * *

One thing that comes up less often in popular culture is Denmark's role in the Atlantic slave trade.

Tens of thousands of enslaved Africans were brought from what is now Ghana to the Danish West Indies before slavery was abolished there in 1848.

Denmark sold these territories to the US in 1917 for a modest $25 million, and you may know them as the US Virgin Islands.

* * *

From 1880 to 1920, more than 350,000 Danes – about 15% of the total population – left Denmark for the US, settling primarily in Wisconsin, Minnesota, Iowa, and the Pacific Northwest.

Denmark was experiencing a population explosion at the time, and there was simply not enough farmland to go around.

The parts of the US to which they moved, usually to work as farmers, resemble Denmark in terrain and climate.

* * *

The country's World War II experience was a complicated one. When Denmark was invaded by the Germans in 1940, the small country's leaders realized that they would not be able to fight the Nazis – who were then at the peak of their power – and surrendered quickly.

Denmark was occupied for five years, although the Danes did a good job of helping many Jews escape to neutral Sweden.

While a Danish resistance movement sabotaged the occupying German forces, a few thousand Danes also volunteered to fight on the German side.

* * *

The 1960s and 1970s were a time of change in Denmark. The welfare state grew quickly. Hundreds of day care centers, hospitals, schools, and nursing homes were built, and many social and class barriers broke down.

Even the Danish language changed noticeably, with the formal version of "you" – familiar to speakers of French, Spanish, and German – mostly disappearing.

In 1967, Denmark became the first country in the world to legalize pornography, which led to a thriving trade in X-rated films and magazines.

At the same time, a strong feminist movement emerged, which means you'll probably never hear a cat call in Denmark unless it comes from a foreigner.

It was also during these decades that Denmark began inviting "guest workers" from Turkey to work in Danish industry, its first step into non-European immigration.

Today, one out of five children born in Denmark has at least one parent who is not an ethnic Dane.

About the Author

Kay Xander Mellish is a speaker, writer, and cultural coach based in Copenhagen, Denmark.

A native of Wauwatosa, Wisconsin, Kay studied journalism and art history at New York University. She worked for several US Fortune 500 companies including units of Disney, News Corp., and Time-Warner before moving to Denmark, where she was employed by Carlsberg and Danske Bank.

This is Kay's fifth book, and a companion volume to her previous book, *Working with Americans: Tips for Danes.*

Kay's first book, *How to Live in Denmark: An entertaining guide for newcomers and their Danish friends,* was based on her long-running podcast and is for sale at Denmark's National Museum.

Kay's book *How to Work in Denmark: Tips on succeeding at work and understanding your Danish boss* has been ordered in bulk by several large Danish companies for distribution to their newly-arrived international specialists.

You can bulk order copies of Kay's books or book Kay for consulting or speeches at www.kxmgroup.dk.

Acknowledgments

Thank you to my advance readers
for their invaluable input.

• • •

Nate Jones, Barbara Erazo-Nielsen,
Joshua Strebel, Paul Leung,
Kimberly Bent, Judith & Don Mellish,
Anita Ågerup Jervelund, Ken Cordes,
Heidi Thisgaard, Chandre Torpet